# FESTIVAL!

## Diwali

Olivia Bennett

# Contents

The Commonwealth [...] as the United Kingdo[...] understanding of the countries and values of the Commonwealth, through education, exhibitions and the arts.

Education programmes have been offered to well over 100 000 children at the Institute each year and many more are reached through extramural programmes and publications.

In pursuing its objectives, the Institute has been responsible for a number of new initiatives, none of which has been more rewarding than its Festivals programmes for schools, which enable many hundreds of children to participate in the celebration of some of the Commonwealth's most significant cultural events. We feel strongly that this opportunity should be offered more widely to teachers and children and are delighted to be able to share in this venture with Macmillan. We trust that this publication will be of assistance to those wanting to know more about Britain's increasingly multicultural society and the wider world in which we live.

Director of the Commonwealth Institute

M Macmillan Education

# Night of a thousand lights

The date of most Indian festivals is fixed using the Indian lunar calendar, which follows the waxing and waning of the moon. Diwali comes during the darkest period of the autumn months, so the lights shine brightly in the moonless night.

▼ Every city, town and village is turned into a fairyland at Diwali, with thousands of tiny lights decorating homes, shops and public buildings.

Picture your home and all the houses nearby at night time. Imagine that it is pitch dark. No bright electric light spills on to the streets from people's windows or street lamps. Instead, by every doorway and along every window sill, there are rows and rows of small flickering lamps. The black night is broken up by hundreds of these tiny pinpricks of light. They give the ordinary-looking houses an almost magical glow. Anyone who has enjoyed the Hindu festival of Diwali will remember a lovely scene like this.

Diwali is a time of new beginnings and of hopes for wealth and happiness to come. Special stories are told and important ideas about good and evil are remembered. It is a time when people are generous and give each other gifts and wear new clothes. There are fairs and family visits to enjoy. But above all, Diwali is a festival of lights.

**Diwas** are the small clay lamps which illuminate people's homes, although today small coloured light bulbs and electric fairy lights are often used. Diwali is Hindi for 'row of lights'. The lights which

This poster shows some of India's annual festivals. Many are religious. Most Indians are Hindu, but there are followers of most world religions in India, including Muslims, Buddhists, Sikhs and Christians. ▶

shine out of the darkness stand for an important idea which Diwali celebrates: that the light of goodness and wisdom is stronger than the darkness of evil and ignorance.

## A year of festivals

Diwali is one of many Hindu festivals. In fact, some say the Indian calendar is really a long list of festivals. Many of these are religious. Some are connected with the seasons, others are just local celebrations. Some festivals celebrate a historical or legendary event, and some are special only to a certain section of Indian society.

Over 680 million people live in India. They follow different religions, speak different languages, and live in a wide range of different landscapes and climates. So it is hardly surprising that there are so many different celebrations – and even different ways of celebrating the same things. Over 500 million Indians are Hindu. Diwali is probably their happiest festival, and the different regions have their own special ways of enjoying it.

3

In some places in India Diwali is a three-day festival, but usually the celebrations last for five days. The first three days come at the end of the Hindu month Asvina, when the nights are dark and moonless. The last two days begin the month of Karttika, when the new moon starts to bring a silvery light back into the sky.

In most parts of the country, the first evening is set aside for worship of Lakshmi, the goddess of wealth and beauty. But the deeds of several Hindu gods and goddesses are celebrated at this time. Different legends are important in different regions.

## The Demon of Filth

In the south of India particularly, people remember a story about Krishna, the god of love, and a horrible demon called Naraka. Naraka never washed or cleaned.

◀ India is a huge country with many different landscapes and climates. To the north are the Himalayan mountains. South of this is the flat and fertile Ganges river basin. The heart of India is the Deccan Plateau. The south is hotter and more tropical.

Indian dancers acting out the ▶ Ramayana, a story of undying love and a battle between good and evil. Diwali celebrates the end of the legend, when the hero Rama returns to his rightful kingdom.

He used to capture beautiful girls and force them to live in his dirty kingdom. Krishna fought and defeated Naraka. As he lay dying, Naraka repented his wicked ways. He asked Krishna if each anniversary of his death could be a time of happiness, so that his death would bring joy to people, even if his life had not. Krishna agreed, and each year people have scented baths, wear new clothes and celebrate the end of the Demon of Filth. One of the women Krishna rescued was Lakshmi. In gratitude she now visits people's homes at Diwali, bringing peace and prosperity.

## The over-ambitious demon king Bali

A story remembered on the fourth day of Diwali is about the god Vishnu's victory over the demon king Bali. Bali was a powerful and very ambitious demon. Not content with controlling the world, he was threatening to take over the heavens too! Vishnu came to earth disguised as a dwarf. He asked Bali to give him as much land as he could cover in three strides. Taken in by the god's disguise, Bali agreed. Imagine his horror when Vishnu grew from a tiny dwarf to a towering giant who covered the entire earth in just two long strides! The demon was punished for his attempts to be god-like by banishment, but he was allowed to return to earth once a year, on the first day of Karttika.

There are other customs and legends connected with Diwali so remember that the pattern of events is not exactly the same for every family or in every region. Perhaps the most well-known reason for celebrating Diwali is Rama's triumphant return to his kingdom, in the final episode of the great Hindu legend, the Ramayana.

# The Ramayana

A statue of Durga, killing an evil ▶ demon, being paraded through city streets. The goddess Durga gave Rama strength to defeat Ravana. So for nine days before Dussehra, there are many celebrations and prayers in her honour, especially in Bengal and other parts of eastern India.

Huge models of Ravana and others ▶▶ are set alight at Dussehra, especially in northern India. Firework displays add excitement to the celebrations of Rama's victory over evil.

◀ An effigy of the demon king Ravana, who kidnaps Rama's beautiful wife, Sita. Eventually, Rama defeats Ravana and rescues Sita. His victory is celebrated at Dussehra.

Diwali comes twenty days after another of India's most popular festivals, Dussehra. This lasts ten days and is closely linked with Diwali because it also celebrates the great Hindu legend called the Ramayana. The final episode of the story belongs to Diwali, but it gets its real meaning from all the events that have taken place earlier.

During Dussehra and up to Diwali, actors perform a cycle of plays called Ram Lila. These tell the story of the Ramayana, and are particularly popular in north India.

## The story

Rama's adventures start when he is exiled into the forest with his beautiful wife Sita, and his loyal brother Lakshmana. Rama was the eldest son of a wise and powerful king, who lived with his three wives and children in the royal city of Ayodhya. One of his wives, to whom he had once promised to grant two wishes, became jealous of Rama. She forced King Dasharatha to appoint her son Bharata as the successor to the throne and to banish Rama from Ayodhya for fourteen years. During their exile in the forest

Rama, Sita and Lakshmana faced many difficulties. The worst episode came when the ten-headed demon king Ravana tricked Rama and Lakshmana into leaving Sita alone. Ravana then snatched her away to his island kingdom of Lanka.

Rama and Lakshmana searched far and wide for poor Sita but with no success. Rama called upon Durga, goddess of motherhood, to give him strength. During the first nine days of Dussehra, people remember this, giving special offerings to Durga, and parading statues of her through the streets.

Eventually, with the help of Hanuman the monkey-warrior, Rama discovered Ravana was keeping Sita in Lanka. Hanuman, Rama, Lakshmana and an army of animals built a bridge across the sea from India to Lanka. Even a little squirrel helped. He rolled in the dust and then trotted off along the bridge to shake the dust from his fur and fill in the cracks between the stones and boulders. The other animals laughed at him but Rama was grateful. He gently stroked the squirrel to show his thanks. From then on, it is said, Indian squirrels had three yellow bands across their backs to show the traces of Rama's fingers.

◀ The Ramayana is often acted out during the festivals of Dussehra and Diwali by actors and actresses wearing masks. Story-teller Rani Singh is playing Hanuman, the monkey god.

At Diwali, the grandest buildings in ▲ ▶ Indian cities are beautifully decorated with rows of shining lights.

After five days the bridge was complete. Rama and Lakshmana crossed over to Lanka. A terrible battle followed but with help from Hanuman and his brave army of monkeys, Rama seemed to be winning. Eventually he and the terrible Ravana met and fought alone. Rama took aim with a magic bow given to him by Durga. He pierced Ravana's huge chest with an arrow which had been made from sunlight and fire. The demon king fell back dead.

This victory is usually celebrated on the last day of Dussehra. Huge models of the demon king are put up in large open spaces. As the sun goes down, a mock battle takes place and the tall figures are set alight by a flaming arrow. As the flames leap into the air, firecrackers hidden inside start to explode. The crowd take part in a spectacular display of fireworks, drumming and dancing.

## The story continues

Victory seemed complete but Rama was uncertain whether Sita had remained true to their love during her terrible ordeal. Sita was so sad when she realised Rama's fears that she longed to die. She prepared a funeral fire. As she walked into the scorching flames, Agni, the god of fire, protected her. When Rama saw her rise unharmed out of the fire, he realised that her love for him had never died. They came together again with great joy.

## The return from exile

By this time, the fourteen years of exile were over, and Rama and Sita journeyed back to Ayodhya. Everyone there greeted their arrival with such happiness! Even Rama's stepmother was glad to see him, for over the years she had become very sorry for what she had done. Her son, Bharata, was delighted, too. He had never felt it was right for him to rule instead of Rama. He had kept a pair of Rama's sandals on the throne all the time, to show who the rightful ruler was. The people of Ayodhya sang, danced and lit all the lamps they could find, and put them in their windows to light Rama and Sita's way home. The shining lights stood for the way goodness and bravery, love and truth had triumphed over wickedness and selfishness.

When Rama and Sita returned to Ayodhya, there was a feeling of new beginnings in the kingdom. Some say the goddess Lakshmi came to Ayodhya at this time, bringing peace and prosperity.

# New beginnings

Families may set up a small shrine to Lakshmi at Diwali. This woman is putting a dot of red scented paste on Lakshmi's forehead as a sign of blessing. Beside the picture of Lakshmi are some of Rama, Sita and other characters in the Ramayana.

◄ Lakshmi, the goddess of wealth and beauty. All gods are partnered by a goddess. Lakshmi is Vishnu's wife. She is believed to have come to earth as Sita when Vishnu took on the form of Rama in order to free the world from evil Ravana.

This feeling of a fresh start and of hopes for a good future is an important part of Diwali. The festival comes just after India's rainy season, which lasts from June to September. Traditionally mustard oil was burnt in the small clay diwas. It helped to clear out the damp monsoon air. Homes are given a good clean and often a fresh coat of paint.

## Lakshmi

This idea of hopes for the future is given more shape by the custom that the first night of Diwali is usually devoted to Lakshmi, goddess of wealth. Families may create a small shrine to Lakshmi at home, by surrounding a statue or picture of her with decorations, flowers and fruits, coloured lights and candles. They place small lamps carefully at their freshly swept and cleaned doorways and windows, hoping to entice Lakshmi in so that she blesses them with wealth and success in the months to come. Lakshmi is said to pass by any dirty or dark, unlit homes.

## The new year

This part of the Diwali celebrations is especially important to traders and business people. Some regard Diwali as the start of a new financial year. People add up their balance sheets, close the old

Diwali comes at the end of October and beginning of November. Kali, the goddess of strength who kills evil, is also worshipped during the festival, particularly in Bengal. Legend says she was born at this time.

account books, and open new ones. Those who have had a good year give offerings to Lakshmi with thanks. Those who have ended up in debt pray that Lakshmi will bless them with more success in the year to come. Over the Diwali holiday, much gambling takes place as those in debt try to make enough to pay off what they owe!

There's a story behind the custom of gambling, too. The god Shiva and his wife Parvati became so obsessed with playing dice they couldn't stop. Vishnu turned himself into some dice for a game which Parvati lost. She was about to curse the dice when she realised it was Vishnu! So she quickly changed her words into a blessing on all those who play dice at this time.

## Kali

In eastern India, especially Bengal, Kali is worshipped. Kali is the goddess of strength who destroys evil. She is another form of Durga, who gave Rama strength in his battle against Ravana. Many statues or pictures show her as fierce and frightening with a necklace of skulls. Bengalis carry huge statues of her through the streets of Calcutta and down to the banks of the River Hooghly to float away on the water.

11

# One God, many faces

This temple statue shows Durga, ▶ goddess of strength, riding a fierce lion. To her right are statues of Brahma (with four heads) and Ganesh (in the foreground) and on her left is Hanuman the monkey god, who stands for loyalty.

◀ Ganesh, god of good fortune, with Lakshmi. Ganesh is a favourite god to whom people pray for good luck – when taking exams, for example, or starting a business.

Ganesh, the elephant-headed god of wisdom and good fortune, is especially popular with Hindus. Many of the pictures of Lakshmi sold at Diwali show him as well. Often these two are accompanied by Saraswati, the goddess of music and learning.

The different gods and goddesses mentioned so far all have a different power and character. They each stand for some of the many powers and qualities of the one great God whom Hindus believe created the world and everything in it. The Hindu name for this one supreme power or spirit is Brahman. Hindus feel that trying to describe God using ordinary human words and ideas is not really possible. God has no shape or form which can be described or shown. God is the life and energy in all living things. God is the power behind nature, which causes rain to fall and rivers to flow. God is in everything and everyone.

It is hard to worship something so difficult to picture or imagine. Most Hindus come closer to God through worship of the many lesser gods and goddesses, which show God's different faces. They are like signposts pointing the way to God. They give shape or form to an idea which is otherwise very hard to see or understand.

Perhaps one way of understanding this idea of the different faces of one God is to think for a moment about someone you know very well. Your mum, for example, shows different faces to different people. She's mother to you, but to various other people, she may be a sister, a daughter, and a wife. She's a friend to some people and a work-mate to others. All of them see her slightly differently.

What about your teacher? Have you ever seen him or her out of school, with some friends or family? You might have been surprised to see them being a different kind of person and showing another side to their character to the one you know at school.

13

# The cycle of life

A Hindu shrine set in a factory wall. It ▶ is not necessary for a Hindu to go to a temple to worship God. Much worship takes place at home, at a family shrine, or at one of India's millions of small road-side shrines like this one.

Although Hindus respect all living ▶▶ creatures, the cow is especially sacred. She produces milk, gives birth to bullocks, which can pull ploughs and heavy carts, and her dung provides manure for fields and fuel for fires.

◀ A modern Hindu temple. People visit temples in India to offer prayers to God at any time.

There are three particularly important Hindu gods. Brahma is the creator (not to be confused with Brahman). Vishnu is the keeper, or preserver, of life. It is believed that Vishnu has come to earth in different forms at certain times. One of these was when he came in the form of Rama, to help save the world from the evil Ravana. Krishna is also a form of Vishnu. Can you think of another story in which Vishnu appears in disguise?

The third main god is Shiva, the destroyer. Old things have to die to make way for new life. So Shiva's destructive powers also lead to creation. He stands for the cycle of life in which birth, death, re-birth and new life follow on from each other.

This idea of the cycle of life is very important in Hinduism. Hindus believe that when living things die, it is only the body which ceases to exist. The spirit never dies but returns to earth in another physical form. The aim is eventually to come so close to God that the soul is freed from this cycle of life. This is called **moksha**. With each rebirth one gets closer, but a soul may go through many bodies and a lot of history before moksha is reached.

This means that Hindus feel our actions in life are very important,

because the way we behave affects the shape of the next life to come. The soul of a cruel or selfish person is likely to return to earth in a form much further away from moksha.

## Karma

This belief that the results of our actions affect our future lives is called **Karma**. It means that Hindus have a strong feeling of responsibility to behave well to all life on earth – not just family and friends but all living things, from the smallest insect upwards. Many Hindus are vegetarian. In particular, Hindus will not eat beef, for the cow is felt to be sacred.

## Hindu worship

Much worship is done at home, at a family shrine dedicated to one or more favourite gods. The act of worship and prayer is called **puja**.

The statues and pictures of the gods and goddesses are treated with great honour and respect. Usually their appearance and the objects they hold are clues to the part of God's character they stand for. For example, Lakshmi holds jewels or money. Saraswati, goddess of music and learning, holds a book and a musical instrument. Brahma has four heads, to show that he has a mind which thinks on all things.

▲ Tourists visit the ancient city of Mohenjo-Daro in the Indus Valley, Pakistan. In the background are the remains of the Great Stupa, a place of worship. Some of the images found in the Indus Valley are similar to modern Hindu gods.

## Temples and shrines

Hindus also worship in temples, although there is no regular gathering for a service of worship. Generally, a temple is seen as a home for the spirit of God which people can visit at any time. Some may go often, others may only worship at home.

However, in Hindu communities outside India or Nepal, temples may become more of a meeting place where local Hindus do gather together for worship on a special day. This is so in Britain, for example.

India and Nepal are also full of small roadside shrines, where worshippers can stop for a few moments' peaceful prayer or make a simple offering of a freshly picked flower, fruit or some grains of rice.

At festival times, the temple courtyards are often crowded with people waiting to go in to the shrine room and worship. Most Diwali celebrations take place at home, but other festivals may involve hundreds of people visiting a particular temple or holy place.

# Indian history

▶ The history of the Indian sub-continent is a story of the rise and fall of many different empires. These are remains of objects made and used by people between the 13th and 8th century BC, when the Aryans ruled much of India.

Most of these festivals will have been celebrated for thousands of years, for Hinduism is one of the world's oldest religions. Nobody can say exactly when it began but some Hindu ideas go as far back as India's first great civilisations. These flourished over 4500 years ago. The ruins of two great cities which existed then have been found in the Punjab and the Indus Valley. The remains tell us that the people who lived then were very good at making things. They had temples, private baths and houses of several storeys.

About a thousand years later, India was invaded by the Aryan people.

Their language developed into Sanskrit, the language of Hindu prayer and worship. They had gods representing the earth, the sun and almost every other form of nature. They brought with them some of the oldest sacred writings that we know of. These are called the **Vedas** and contain important Hindu beliefs. As the centuries went by, more sacred books were written. A system developed which divided people into different groups called castes. As the religious beliefs developed and ceremonies became more complicated, the power of the priests, who were the highest caste, grew.

17

# Diwali

◀ Sri Lankan Buddhists at worship. One of India's greatest rulers, Ashoka, became a Buddhist. He spread the Buddha's teachings all over his large Indian empire and into Sri Lanka and other lands.

A Rajput palace, Jaipur. The warrior ▶ Rajput princes resisted the Mughal Emperors who ruled much of India in the 16th century. The Mughals themselves built many beautifully decorated mosques and palaces.

Throughout early Indian history, empires rose and fell in different parts of this huge land. The Aryans were followed by the Greek empire of Alexander the Great. He was followed by the Mauryan emperors.

While all these changes were going on, an important religious thinker and leader appeared. He was called the Buddha. He taught that the suffering in the world was caused by people's greed and selfishness. If people would give up always wanting the wrong things in life, they could find peace and understanding.

One of the greatest of the Mauryan emperors, called Ashoka, became a Buddhist. For nearly a thousand years, Buddhism was a very important religion in India. After Ashoka's death, his empire collapsed and a series of smaller kingdoms gained and lost power. One of these, the Gupta kingdom, was a golden age of great achievements in art, science and mathematics.

Buddhism remained important but more and more people were beginning to follow the earlier religious beliefs and practices, which later came to be called Hinduism. At this time two great poems were written. One was the Ramayana, which is retold before and during Diwali each year. The

▲ One of the Mughals, Shah Jehan, built the lovely Taj Mahal in memory of his wife, Mumtaz Mahal.

other was the Mahabharata, which explains many important Hindu beliefs.

## Islam and India

From the 7th century AD, another empire was gaining strength. It was the Islamic religious empire and it was to have a powerful effect on the story of India. A century later, its followers began to invade north India. Like the Aryans and Greeks before them, the Muslims brought their own customs, culture and beliefs. Once again, these became part of Indian life and history. From the 16th century, the Muslim rulers known as Mughals held power. India was one of the richest and most powerful countries in the world.

From the end of the 15th century, European powers became interested in India's riches. The Mughal empire eventually collapsed. British, Dutch, Portuguese and French forces all competed for India's wealth, but the British finally ruled the country.

India won independence in 1947. The country was divided into India and Pakistan (part of Pakistan later became Bangladesh). The fighting which followed this partition, as Hindus and Muslims fled to the different states, was one of the saddest episodes in Indian history.

# India today

▲ India is a land of contrasts and of great natural beauty. Most of her people make their living from the land, farming a variety of landscapes. Life in the steep mountain valleys of the Himalayas is very different from that in the fertile plains of the Ganges River Basin.

Since independence, India has achieved a great deal. She now grows enough grain to feed her huge population, something which many other countries have not yet managed. She has become one of the world's largest industrial powers. Yet many challenges remain. The country has suffered fighting between Indians of different caste and religion. The majority of the ever-growing population are very poor.

## Contrasts

So India is a country of contrasts. A land where the way of life in many villages has hardly changed for hundreds of years, yet which has its own space programme.

Recently, the first Indian astronaut was sent into space. Part of his job was to take special photographs which would show where oil and other resources lie hidden in the soil and seas of India. If his camera had been able to zoom in on the scenes of ordinary life taking place millions of miles below him, what would he have seen?

India is above all a land of villages, for most of her population make their living from the land. So the astronaut would have seen thousands of small

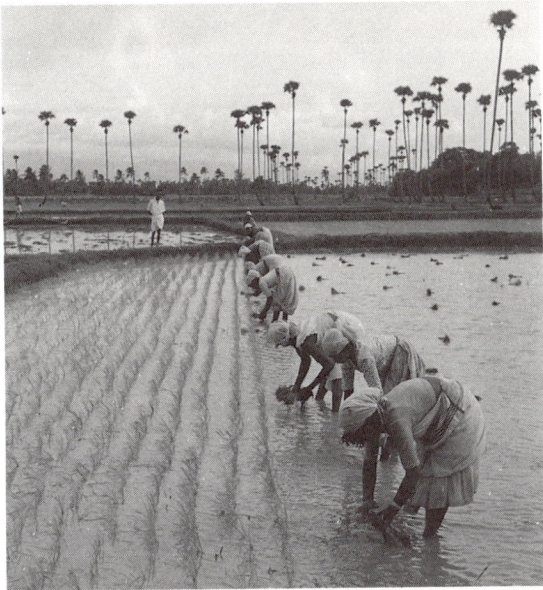

▼ Rice makes up the bulk of many an Indian diet, especially in the more tropical south. In the north, wheat is more common and is made into many different kinds of bread.

▲ As well as geographical contrasts, India is a land where the old and new still exist together. Fishermen using methods unchanged for hundreds of years may work next to a busy modern port with oil refineries and factories producing the latest machinery.

country towns and villages, some perched on steep mountainsides, others sprawled along palm-fringed beaches, some surrounded by thick forest and others like lonely dots on vast dry plains and deserts. Many villages lie in the midst of the brilliant green paddy fields of India's river plains, where heavy water buffaloes pull ploughs through fertile fields, and women thresh rice in ways unchanged for generations.

He would have seen thousands of temples, many dotted along the banks of India's large rivers, which wind their way down to busy modern ports surrounded by steel plants, factories and oil refineries. India today produces most of the goods her vast population needs, and her industry is growing all the time. And as it does, people are leaving the countryside to find work in the cities.

Already India has some of the world's biggest cities. Beside the skyscrapers and smart hotels of the city centres lie huge squatter settlements, where families live in one or two rooms and share a water tap with many others. Yet if the astronaut looked closely, he would see people working hard to improve these settlements, laying water pipes, building schools, and starting small businesses.

# Diwali

▲ The majority of India's people make their living from the land but more and more are moving to the cities where they feel their children have a better chance of going to school and finding work.

▼ One of the ways many families decorate their homes for Diwali is with floor patterns like these, called rangoli.

If the spacecraft had drifted over these cities during Diwali, the astronaut would have seen grand buildings decorated with garlands of coloured lights. Even the smallest slum dwelling would be transformed by the golden glow of candlelight as families pray to Lakshmi for her blessing.

The old and new live alongside each other in Indian cities. Motor cars squeeze through crowded streets, overtaking creaking bullock carts piled high with fresh vegetables and fruit. Everyone, whether driving bus, lorry, car, rickshaw or cart, takes care to avoid the cows which amble slowly through the tangle of traffic. Food markets are full of fruit, vegetables, grains and spices of every colour, taste, smell and texture you could imagine. The variety of Indian food is enormous, although for the poor there is little choice. Every region has its cooking specialities, in some areas based around rice as the staple food and in others around wheat.

# Diwali customs

▶ The floor decorations are usually made with coloured rice-flour paste, or powdered chalks or spices. These patterns are being painted at a demonstration of different designs.

For many familes Diwali is a time when everyone tries to get together and share food, news and gifts. Sometimes on the last day sisters give their brothers a special feast or party. The food eaten at the festivities will be different all over India, but most people follow the custom of exchanging gifts of sweets at Diwali. Sweet shops fill their windows with pyramids of different coloured sweets, some decorated with thin silver paper which can be eaten. Most sweets are made from boiled milk and sugar and are flavoured with all kinds of nuts, fruit, raisins, or rosewater. During Diwali pavement stalls sell puffed rice, roasted corn and cheap sweets made from spun sugar, so that even the poorest people can give and receive large quantities of Diwali sweets.

One of the things which families do to make their homes beautiful in the hope of attracting Lakshmi's blessing is to make floor patterns called **rangoli**. In the Gujarat region this is an especially important part of Diwali preparations. The designs are built up from curved shapes or from geometric patterns. Traditionally women make the rangoli. They use coloured pastes of rice-flour and water, or dry powders such as ground-up chalks or spices.

# Diwali

▼ It has become the custom for friends and families to send each other Diwali cards. The greeting inside these is 'Happy Diwali and best wishes for happiness in the year to come.'

▶ Hindus in Malaysia and the Indonesian island of Bali retell the Ramayana story using traditional shadow puppets.

Another Diwali custom is the sending of cards. Often these have pictures of Lakshmi, or drawings of lamps. The greeting inside is usually Subh Diwali, (Happy Diwali). Friends and families pay each other visits. As well as exchanging gifts of sweets, other presents are given, especially of new clothes or small amounts of money. Families also give small presents to any people who work for them, such as a gardener.

Business people may visit clients and customers, hoping to start the new financial year on a good note. It's the start of a new farming year, too. The end of the monsoon rains means it is time to start planting seed for the next harvest.

And of course there are performances and readings of the Ramayana, especially in north India. In Malaysia, the Hindu community use the delicate shadow puppets which are traditionally used for storytelling there. In Bali, shadow puppets are also used. Story-telling sessions last well into the night to the tinkling sound of beautiful Balinese music.

# Sikhs and Diwali

▼ The Sikh's Golden Temple at Amritsar is decorated with thousands of lights at Diwali.

Diwali is also celebrated by Sikhs, followers of a religion which was founded by Guru Nanak in India about 500 years ago. Guru means a guide or teacher. Guru Nanak was born a Hindu but grew up in a Muslim community. He wished Sikhism to be a faith which united people in their search for God. He was followed by nine more gurus, the last of whom died in 1708. Sikhism had many followers by this time. The last guru appointed the Sikh's holy book as the next guru. He felt that it contained all the teachings of Sikhism and therefore Sikhs did not need a human teacher any more.

From then on the book was called the Guru Granth Sahib.

Guru Nanak had hoped to stop much of the quarrelling and suspicion which sometimes divides people of different faiths, but at times Sikhs themselves have had to fight for their beliefs. The sixth guru was imprisoned by the Mughal Emperor Jehangir. He was finally released at Diwali, so it is a time of great happiness for Sikhs. Their beautiful Golden Temple at Amritsar is decorated with hundreds of small lights which are reflected in the lake which surrounds it.

25

# Diwali mela

▲ A street trader sells garlands of fresh flowers with which people decorate statues of gods and goddesses at Diwali, as well as the entrances to their shops and homes.

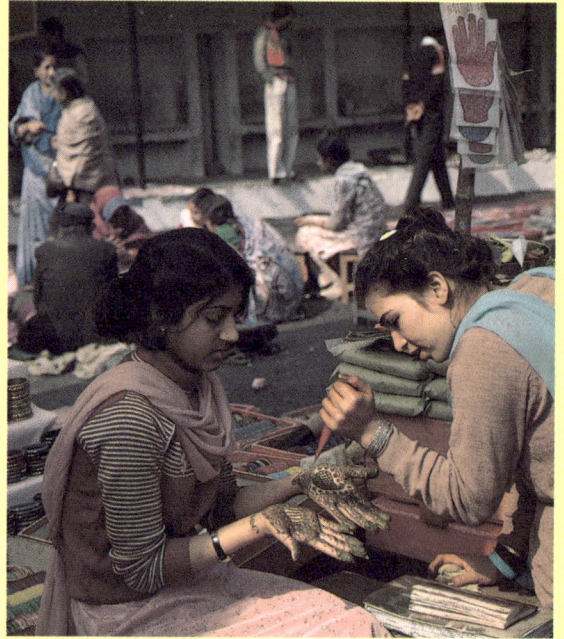

▲ For festivals and special occasions, women have patterns painted on their hands with henna.

Indian festivals are often the excuse for a fair and Diwali is no exception. The Hindi word for fair is **mela**. A mela often serves as a market as well, particularly in the country. Villagers can buy and sell animals and farm produce, and exchange news and gossip. Travelling tradesmen take advantage of the crowds to sell brightly coloured materials, clothes, books, toys and all sorts of goods brought from the city.

Best of all, the mela is full of delicious things to eat and exciting things to look at or do. Entertainers, from snake charmers and fortune tellers to jugglers and acrobats, mingle with the crowds. Excited children scramble for rides on elephants and swaying camels. Big wheels spin round with shrieking children hanging on for dear life.

Bangle sellers at the mela do great business at Diwali. Their stalls display rows and rows of coloured, shiny glass bangles. Girls and women choose lots of these pretty bracelets to mix and match with their new Diwali clothes.

Food stalls keep going all day, selling hot and spicy, or sweet and

▼ Bangle sellers do good business at Diwali time, as girls and women buy lots of coloured bracelets to match their new Diwali clothes.

sticky snacks. Tea, fruit juices and soft drinks are also sold. Other stalls sell Diwali decorations and pictures of Lakshmi and other gods and goddesses. Groups of men sit hunched on their heels around packs of cards, gambling fast and hoping for Lakshmi's blessing. There are puppet shows and lots of music and dancing. One dance, the garba, is traditionally danced by Gujarati girls at Diwali melas.

At other stalls, women have beautiful and delicate designs painted in henna on their hands. Henna is a brown dye made from a plant. Many women and girls wear gold jewellery and are dressed in red, the colour of luck and good fortune.

Night falls and excitement mounts as the high point of the Diwali mela is reached. A huge firework display is set off. Popping firecrackers, swooshing rockets and exploding stars of silver, gold and all the colours of the rainbow light up the vast Indian sky. Exhausted children finally go to bed, the sound of fireworks ringing in their ears – a sure sign that Diwali is here again.

# Diwali in Britain

On the Saturday or Sunday morning ▶ closest to Diwali, many British Hindus go to their local temple to worship together. The priest at this South London temple said prayers for them and placed flower petals on the shrine.

▼ The family pray together in front of the shrine to Lakshmi which they have made for Diwali. On the table they have put sweets, incense, fruits, lights and a conch shell.

▲ A British Hindu family decorate their front step with small Diwali lamps.

Apart from India, only in Nepal and the Indonesian island of Bali is Hinduism the main religion. Yet there are more followers of Hinduism in Asia than any other religion. Diwali has always been one of their favourite festivals. It is remembered and celebrated by Hindu communities wherever they live. In Britain, for example, it is probably the Hindu festival that non-Hindus know most about, and may have been invited to join in. Many schools with Hindu pupils enjoy putting on a play which retells the story of Rama's rescue of Sita and their return to Ayodhya. For some schools it has become an annual event.

Of course, there are no huge Diwali melas to enjoy, but many British Hindu families brighten up their homes with Diwali cards and decorations. Families and friends visit each other and exchange sweets, food and other gifts. The windows of Indian sweetshops in Britain are usually especially full of sweets of every shape, flavour and colour at this time.

November in Britain is often cold, damp and windy. Leaving small lamps on window sills or by open doorways is not always possible, but the diwas still play their part in creating the atmosphere of Diwali in the home.

A shrine to Lakshmi may be set up, and offerings of fruit and sweets placed in front of her statue or picture. Some families may give a firework party in the garden, where children play with sparklers which hiss and spit their tiny silver stars into the damp English night.

Diwali is not a public holiday as it is in India or Nepal, but on the nearest Saturday or Sunday people may gather together to worship at their local Hindu temple. A temple used mostly by families who originally came from Bengal may have a statue of Durga or Kali in pride of place, surrounded by pictures of Rama, Sita, Hanuman and other gods. In other temples, a special shrine will be devoted to Lakshmi.

Diwali is more of an indoor celebration in Britain. In India the rains have at last stopped, the nights are warm and dry and so everyone is out in the streets celebrating. Even busy city streets are less full of traffic and are safer for children, because everyone is celebrating the same event.

# Diwali elsewhere

Temples in the parts of Britain, the West Indies and East Africa where Hindus have settled are often meeting places for the local Hindu community. ▶

Lighting Diwali lamps in Trinidad. ▶▶ Wherever Diwali is celebrated, the glow of the lights reminds people of the power of goodness and truth to shine more brightly than evil and selfish deeds.

◀ A Hindu temple in Singapore. There are more Hindus than followers of any other religion in Asia. Diwali is one of their happiest festivals. It is celebrated by Hindu communities all over the world.

In India's long history, many different peoples have held power and then given way to others. Each time the Indian continent seemed to soak up certain customs and traditions of these civilisations and turn them into something very special to India. And Indians and their culture have in turn influenced other lands and people, too. The English language, for example, now contains many words which entered British speech and way of life after British rule in India. Hindu beliefs and ideas have affected western thinking.

## The Caribbean

In recent centuries many Indians have left their homeland and settled elsewhere in search of work. One movement like this was to the Caribbean. It took place in the nineteenth century. The landowners there had depended on African slaves to work on their sugar plantations. When the slave trade was abolished, most of the Africans left the plantations. The landowners found workers to replace them in east India, especially Bengal. The demand was great, particularly in Trinidad and Guyana. Unlike the slaves, the

east Indians only had to work a number of years on the plantations and then they were free to settle or return home. Most did settle there, and many were Hindu.

Today, Hindu customs, music and religion flourish in Trinidad and in other Caribbean countries. There are many temples to Shiva, Vishnu and other gods and goddesses. Hindu festivals are celebrated with great enthusiasm. At Diwali, villages are dotted with clusters of glowing lamps and candles, and Hindu music floats out of people's homes into the warm Caribbean night.

## East Africa

Many Indians from the Gujarat region of India moved to East Africa and settled there. They were particularly successful in trade and business. And just as Hindu customs and festivals in Trinidad have a Bengali flavour, so Gujarati ways of doing things survived in East Africa.

But wherever Diwali is celebrated, the overall feeling is one of happiness and generosity. The diwa lamps are a powerful reminder of how truth and goodness can win through the blackness of evil and wickedness.

# Acknowledgements

The author and publishers would like to thank Urvashi Butalia and Owen Cole for their help in the preparation of this book.

The author and publishers wish to acknowledge the following photographic sources:
Olivia Bennett, pages 2, 26, 27
Central Office of Information, page 5
Steve Harrison, page 12
Governement of India Tourist Office, London, pages 8, 9, 20, 21, 25
Pakistan Embassy, London, pages 16, 17
Liba Taylor, pages 11, 13, 28, 29, 31
N. Thiagarajan, pages 3, 6, 7

The remaining photographs used in this book were provided by the Commonwealth Institute.

© Olivia Bennett 1986

First published 1986
Reprinted 1987

Published by
MACMILLAN EDUCATION LTD
Houndmills, Basingstoke, Hampshire RG21 2XS
and London
Companies and representatives
throughout the world

Designed by
The Tandem Design Company, Reading

Printed in Hong Kong

ISBN 0-333-37899-7